BEWARE OF PRIDE

and

THE BOOK OF MORMON— KEYSTONE OF OUR RELIGION

D1604094

BEWARE OF PRIDE

and

THE BOOK OF MORMON— KEYSTONE OF OUR RELIGION

Ezra Taft Benson

CLASSIC TALK SERIES

Deseret Book Company
Salt Lake City, Utah

Reprinted with permission.

Library of Congress Catalog Card Number: 97-078184
ISBN 0-87579-881-0

Printed in the United States of America

10   9   8   7   6   5   4   3   2   1   72082

BEWARE OF PRIDE

My beloved brethren and sisters, I rejoice to be with you in another glorious general conference of the Church. How grateful I am for the love, prayers, and service of the devoted members of the Church throughout the world.

May I commend you faithful Saints who are striving to flood the earth and your lives with the Book of Mormon. Not only must we move forward in a monumental manner more copies of the Book of Mormon, but we must move

1

boldly forward into our own lives and throughout the earth more of its marvelous messages.

This sacred volume was written for us—for
our day. Its scriptures are to be likened unto ourselves (see 1 Nephi 19:23).

The Doctrine and Covenants tells us that the
Book of Mormon is the "record of a fallen
people" (D&C 20:9). Why did they fall? This is
one of the major messages of the Book of
Mormon. Mormon gives the answer in the clos-
ing chapters of the book in these words:
"Behold, the pride of this nation, or the people
of the Nephites, hath proven their destruction"
(Moroni 8:27). And then, lest we miss that
momentous Book of Mormon message from that
fallen people, the Lord warns us in the Doctrine
and Covenants, "Beware of pride, lest ye
become as the Nephites of old" (D&C 38:39).

I earnestly seek an interest in your faith and
prayers as I strive to bring forth light on this

Book of Mormon message—the sin of pride. This message has been weighing heavily on my soul for some time. I know the Lord wants this message delivered now.

In the premortal council, it was pride that felled Lucifer, "a son of the morning" (2 Nephi 24:12–15; see also D&C 76:25–27; Moses 4:3). At the end of this world, when God cleanses the earth by fire, the proud will be burned as stubble and the meek shall inherit the earth (see 3 Nephi 12:5; 25:1; D&C 29:9; Joseph Smith–History 1:37; Malachi 4:1).

Three times in the Doctrine and Covenants the Lord uses the phrase "beware of pride," including a warning to the second elder of the Church, Oliver Cowdery, and to Emma Smith, the wife of the Prophet (D&C 23:1; see also 25:14; 38:39).

Pride is a very misunderstood sin, and many are sinning in ignorance (see Mosiah 3:11;

3 Nephi 6:18). In the scriptures there is no such thing as righteous pride—it is always considered a sin. Therefore, no matter how the world uses the term, we must understand how God uses the term so we can understand the language of holy writ and profit thereby (see 2 Nephi 4:15; Mosiah 1:3–7; Alma 5:61).

Most of us think of pride as self-centeredness, conceit, boastfulness, arrogance, or haughtiness. All of these are elements of the sin, but the heart, or core, is still missing.

The central feature of pride is enmity—enmity toward God and enmity toward our fellowmen. *Enmity* means "hatred toward, hostility to, or a state of opposition." It is the power by which Satan wishes to reign over us.

Pride is essentially competitive in nature. We pit our will against God's. When we direct our pride toward God, it is in the spirit of "my will and not thine be done." As Paul said, they "seek their own, not the things which are Jesus Christ's" (Philippians 2:21).

Our will in competition to God's will allows desires, appetites, and passions to go unbridled (see Alma 38:12; 3 Nephi 12:30).

The proud cannot accept the authority of God giving direction to their lives (see Helaman 12:6). They pit their perceptions of truth against God's great knowledge, their abilities versus God's priesthood power, their accomplishments against His mighty works.

Our enmity toward God takes on many labels, such as rebellion, hard-heartedness, stiff-neckedness, unrepentant, puffed up, easily offended, and sign seekers. The proud wish God would agree with them. They aren't interested in changing their opinions to agree with God's.

Another major portion of this very prevalent sin of pride is enmity toward our fellowmen. We are tempted daily to elevate ourselves above others and diminish them (see Helaman 6:17; D&C 58:41).

The proud make every man their adversary by pitting their intellects, opinions, works, wealth, talents, or any other worldly measuring device against others. In the words of C. S. Lewis: "Pride gets no pleasure out of having something, only out of having more of it than the next man. . . . It is the comparison that makes you proud: the pleasure of being above the rest. Once the element of competition has gone, pride has gone" (*Mere Christianity*, New York: Macmillan, 1952, 109–10).

In the pre-earthly council, Lucifer placed his proposal in competition with the Father's plan as advocated by Jesus Christ (see Moses 4:1–3). He wished to be honored above all others (see 2 Nephi 24:13). In short, his prideful desire was to dethrone God (see D&C 29:36; 76:28).

The scriptures abound with evidences of the

severe consequences of the sin of pride to individuals, groups, cities, and nations. "Pride goeth before destruction" (Proverbs 16:18). It destroyed the Nephite nation and the city of Sodom (see Moroni 8:27; Ezekiel 16:49–50).

It was through pride that Christ was crucified. The Pharisees were wroth because Jesus claimed to be the Son of God, which was a threat to their position, and so they plotted His death (see John 11:53).

Saul became an enemy to David through pride. He was jealous because the crowds of Israelite women were singing that "Saul hath slain his thousands, and David his ten thousands" (1 Samuel 18:6–8).

The proud stand more in fear of men's judgment than of God's judgment (see D&C 3:6–7; 30:1–2; 60:2). "What will men think of me?" weighs heavier than "What will God think of me?"

King Noah was about to free the prophet Abinadi, but an appeal to his pride by his wicked priests sent Abinadi to the flames (see Mosiah 17:11–12). Herod sorrowed at the request of his wife to behead John the Baptist, but his prideful desire to look good to "them which sat with him at meat" caused him to kill John (Matthew 14:9; see also Mark 6:26).

Fear of men's judgment manifests itself in competition for men's approval. The proud love "the praise of men more than the praise of God" (John 12:42–43). Our motives for the things we do are where the sin is manifest. Jesus said He did "always those things" that pleased God (John 8:29). Would we not do well to have the pleasing of God as our motive rather than to try to elevate ourselves above our brother and outdo another?

Some prideful people are not so concerned as to whether their wages meet their needs as they are that their wages are more than someone else's. Their reward is being a cut above the rest. This is the enmity of pride.

When pride has a hold on our hearts, we lose our independence of the world and deliver our freedoms to the bondage of men's judgment. The world shouts louder than the whisperings of the Holy Ghost. The reasoning of men overrides the revelations of God, and the proud let go of the iron rod (see 1 Nephi 8:19–28; 11:25; 15:23–24).

Pride is a sin that can readily be seen in others but is rarely admitted in ourselves. Most of us consider pride to be a sin of those on the top, such as the rich and the learned, looking down at the rest of us (see 2 Nephi 9:42). There is, however, a far more common ailment among us— and that is pride from the bottom looking up. It is manifest in so many ways, such as faultfinding, gossiping, backbiting, murmuring, living

beyond our means, envying, coveting, with-
holding gratitude and praise that might lift
another, and being unforgiving and jealous.

Disobedience is essentially a prideful power
struggle against someone in authority over us. It
can be a parent, a priesthood leader, a teacher, or
ultimately God. A proud person hates the fact
that someone is above him. He thinks this low-
ers his position.

Selfishness is one of the more common faces
of pride. "How everything affects me" is the
center of all that matters—self-conceit, self-pity,
worldly self-fulfillment, self-gratification, and
self-seeking.

Pride results in secret combinations which are
built up to get power, gain, and glory of the
world (see Helaman 7:5; Ether 8:9, 16, 22–23;
Moses 5:31). This fruit of the sin of pride, namely
secret combinations, brought down both the
Jaredite and the Nephite civilizations and has

been and will yet be the cause of the fall of many nations (see Ether 8:18–25).

Another face of pride is contention. Arguments, fights, unrighteous dominion, generation gaps, divorces, spouse abuse, riots, and disturbances all fall into this category of pride.

Contention in our families drives the Spirit of the Lord away. It also drives many of our family members away. Contention ranges from a hostile spoken word to worldwide conflicts. The scriptures tell us that "only by pride cometh contention" (Proverbs 13:10; see also Proverbs 28:25).

The scriptures testify that the proud are easily offended and hold grudges (see 1 Nephi 16:1–3). They withhold forgiveness to keep another in their debt and to justify their injured feelings.

The proud do not receive counsel or correction easily (see Proverbs 15:10; Amos 5:10). Defensiveness is used by them to justify and rationalize their frailties and failures (see Matthew 3:9; John 6:30–59).

The proud depend upon the world to tell them whether they have value or not. Their self-esteem is determined by where they are judged to be on the ladders of worldly success. They feel worthwhile as individuals if the numbers beneath them in achievement, talent, beauty, or intellect are large enough. Pride is ugly. It says, "If you succeed, I am a failure."

If we love God, do His will, and fear His judgment more than men's, we will have self-esteem.

Pride is a damning sin in the true sense of that word. It limits or stops progression (see Alma 12:10–11). The proud are not easily taught (see 1 Nephi 15:3, 7–11). They won't change their minds to accept truths, because to do so implies they have been wrong.

Pride adversely affects all our relationships—our relationship with God and His servants, between husband and wife, parent and child, employer and employee, teacher and student, and all mankind. Our degree of pride determines how we treat our God and our brothers and sisters. Christ wants to lift us to where He is. Do we desire to do the same for others?

Pride fades our feelings of sonship to God and brotherhood to man. It separates and divides us by "ranks," according to our "riches" and our "chances for learning" (3 Nephi 6:12). Unity is impossible for a proud people, and unless we are one we are not the Lord's (see Mosiah 18:21; D&C 38:27; 105:2–4; Moses 7:18).

Think of what pride has cost us in the past and what it is now costing us in our own lives, our families, and the Church.

Think of the repentance that could take place with lives changed, marriages preserved, and homes strengthened, if pride did not keep us from confessing our sins and forsaking them (see D&C 58:43).

Think of the many who are less active members of the Church because they were offended and their pride will not allow them to forgive or fully sup at the Lord's table.

Think of the tens of thousands of additional young men and couples who could be on missions except for the pride that keeps them from yielding their hearts unto God (see Alma 10:6; Helaman 3:34–35).

Think how temple work would increase if the time spent in this godly service were more important than the many prideful pursuits that compete for our time.

Pride affects all of us at various times and in various degrees. Now you can see why the building in Lehi's dream that represents the pride of the world was large and spacious and great was the multitude that did enter into it (see 1 Nephi 8:26, 33; 11:35–36).

Pride is the universal sin, the great vice. Yes, pride *is* the universal sin, the great vice.

The antidote for pride is humility—meekness, submissiveness (see Alma 7:23). It is the broken heart and contrite spirit (see 3 Nephi 9:20; 12:19; D&C 20:37; 59:8; Psalm 34:18; Isaiah 57:15; 66:2). As Rudyard Kipling put it so well:

> *The tumult and the shouting dies;*
> *The captains and the kings depart.*
> *Still stands thine ancient sacrifice,*
> *An humble and a contrite heart.*
> *Lord God of Hosts, be with us yet,*
> *Lest we forget, lest we forget.*
> (Hymns, *1985, no. 80*)

God will have a humble people. Either we can choose to be humble or we can be compelled to be humble. Alma said, "Blessed are they who humble themselves without being compelled to be humble" (Alma 32:16).

Let us choose to be humble.

We can choose to humble ourselves by conquering enmity toward our brothers and sisters, esteeming them as ourselves, and lifting them as high or higher than we are (see D&C 38:24; 81:5; 84:106).

We can choose to humble ourselves by receiving counsel and chastisement (see Jacob 4:10; Helaman 15:3; D&C 63:55; 101:4–5; 108:1; 124:61, 84; 136:31; Proverbs 9:8).

We can choose to humble ourselves by forgiving those who have offended us (see 3 Nephi 13:11, 14; D&C 64:10).

We can choose to humble ourselves by rendering selfless service (see Mosiah 2:16–17).

We can choose to humble ourselves by going on missions and preaching the word that can humble others (see Alma 4:19; 31:5; 48:20).

We can choose to humble ourselves by getting to the temple more frequently.

We can choose to humble ourselves by confessing and forsaking our sins and being born of God (see D&C 58:43; Mosiah 27:25–26; Alma 5:7–14, 49).

We can choose to humble ourselves by loving God, submitting our will to His, and putting Him first in our lives (see 3 Nephi 11:11; 13:33; Moroni 10:32).

Let us choose to be humble. We can do it. I know we can.

My dear brethren and sisters, we must prepare to redeem Zion. It was essentially the sin of pride that kept us from establishing Zion in the days of the Prophet Joseph Smith. It was the same sin of pride that brought consecration to an end among the Nephites (see 4 Nephi 1:24–25).

Pride is the great stumbling block to Zion.

I repeat: Pride *is* the great stumbling block to Zion.

We must cleanse the inner vessel by conquering pride (see Alma 6:2–4; Matthew 23:25–26).

We must yield "to the enticings of the Holy Spirit," put off the prideful "natural man," become "a saint through the atonement of Christ the Lord," and become "as a child, submissive, meek, humble" (Mosiah 3:19; see also Alma 13:28).

That we may do so and go on to fulfill our divine destiny is my fervent prayer in the name of Jesus Christ, amen.

From an address given at the April 1989 general conference while President Benson was serving as president of The Church of Jesus Christ of Latter-day Saints (see *Ensign*, May 1989, 4–7).

THE BOOK OF MORMON—
KEYSTONE OF OUR RELIGION

My beloved brethren and sisters, today I would like to speak about one of the most significant gifts given to the world in modern times. The gift I am thinking of is more important than any of the inventions that have come out of the industrial and technological revolutions. This is a gift of greater value to mankind than even the many wonderful advances we have seen in modern medicine. It is of greater worth to mankind than the development of flight or space travel. I speak of the gift of the Book of Mormon, given to mankind 156 years ago.

This gift was prepared by the hand of the Lord over a period of more than a thousand years, then hidden up by Him so that it would be preserved in its purity for our generation. Perhaps there is nothing that testifies more clearly of the importance of this modern book of scripture than what the Lord Himself has said about it.

By His own mouth He has borne witness (1) that it is true (D&C 17:6), (2) that it contains the truth and His words (D&C 19:26), (3) that it was translated by power from on high (D&C 20:8), (4) that it contains the fulness of the gospel of Jesus Christ (D&C 20:9; 42:12), (5) that it was given by inspiration and confirmed by the ministering of angels (D&C 20:10), (6) that it gives evidence that the holy scriptures are true (D&C 20:11), and (7) that those who receive it in faith shall receive eternal life (D&C 20:14).

A second powerful testimony to the importance of the Book of Mormon is to note where the Lord placed its coming forth in the timetable of the unfolding Restoration. The only thing that preceded it was the First Vision. In that marvelous manifestation, the Prophet Joseph Smith learned the true nature of God and that God had a work for him to do. The coming forth of the Book of Mormon was the next thing to follow.

Think of that in terms of what it implies. The coming forth of the Book of Mormon preceded the restoration of the priesthood. It was published just a few days before the Church was organized. The Saints were given the Book of Mormon to read before they were given the revelations outlining such great doctrines as the three degrees of glory, celestial marriage, or work for the dead. It came before priesthood quorums and Church organization. Doesn't this tell us something about how the Lord views this sacred work?

Once we realize how the Lord feels about this book, it should not surprise us that He also gives us solemn warnings about how we receive it. After indicating that those who receive the Book of Mormon with faith, working righteousness, will receive a crown of eternal life (see D&C 20:14), the Lord follows with this warning: "But those who harden their hearts in unbelief, and reject it, it shall turn to their own condemnation" (D&C 20:15).

In 1829, the Lord warned the Saints that they are not to trifle with sacred things (see D&C 6:12). Surely the Book of Mormon is a sacred thing, and yet many trifle with it, or in other words, take it lightly, treat it as though it is of little importance.

In 1832, as some early missionaries returned from their fields of labor, the Lord reproved them for treating the Book of Mormon lightly. As a result of that attitude, He said, their minds had been darkened. Not only had treating this sacred book lightly brought a loss of light to themselves, it had also brought the whole Church under condemnation, even all the children of Zion. And then the Lord said, "And they shall remain under this condemnation until they repent and remember the new covenant, even the Book of Mormon" (D&C 84:54–57).

Has the fact that we have had the Book of Mormon with us for over a century and a half made it seem less significant to us today? Do we remember the new covenant, even the Book of Mormon? In the Bible we have the Old Testament and the New Testament. The word *testament* is the English rendering of a Greek word that can also be translated as *covenant*. Is this what the Lord meant when He called the Book of Mormon the "new covenant"? It is indeed another testament or witness of Jesus. This is one of the reasons why we have recently added the words "Another Testament of Jesus Christ" to the title of the Book of Mormon.

If the early Saints were rebuked for treating the Book of Mormon lightly, are we under any less condemnation if we do the same? The Lord Himself bears testimony that it is of eternal significance. Can a small number of us bring the whole Church under condemnation because we trifle with sacred things? What will we say at the Judgment when we stand before Him and meet His probing gaze if we are among those described as forgetting the new covenant?

There are three great reasons why Latter-day Saints should make the study of the Book of Mormon a lifetime pursuit.

The *first* is that the Book of Mormon is the keystone of our religion. This was the Prophet Joseph Smith's statement. He testified that "the

Book of Mormon was the most correct of any book on earth, and the keystone of our religion" (Introduction to the Book of Mormon). A keystone is the central stone in an arch. It holds all the other stones in place, and if it is removed, the arch crumbles.

There are three ways in which the Book of Mormon is the keystone of our religion. It is the keystone in our witness of Christ. It is the keystone of our doctrine. It is the keystone of testimony.

The Book of Mormon is the keystone in our witness of Jesus Christ, who is Himself the cornerstone of everything we do. It bears witness of His reality with power and clarity. Unlike the Bible, which passed through generations of copyists, translators, and corrupt religionists who tampered with the text, the Book of Mormon came from writer to reader in just one inspired step of translation. Therefore, its testimony of the Master is clear, undiluted, and full of power. But it does even more. Much of the Christian world today rejects the divinity of the Savior. They question His miraculous birth, His perfect life, and the reality of His glorious resurrection. The Book of Mormon teaches in plain and unmistakable terms about the truth of all of those. It also provides the most complete explanation of the doctrine of the Atonement. Truly, this divinely inspired book is a keystone in bearing witness to the world that Jesus is the Christ (see title page of the Book of Mormon).

The Book of Mormon is also the keystone of the doctrine of the Resurrection. As mentioned before, the Lord Himself has stated that the Book of Mormon contains the "fulness of the gospel of Jesus Christ" (D&C 20:9). That does not mean it contains every teaching, every doctrine ever revealed. Rather, it means that in the Book of Mormon we will find the fulness of those doctrines required for our salvation. And they are taught plainly and simply so that even children can learn the ways of salvation and exaltation. The Book of Mormon offers so much that broadens our understandings of the doctrines of salvation. Without it, much of what is taught in other scriptures would not be nearly so plain and precious.

Finally, the Book of Mormon is the keystone of testimony. Just as the arch crumbles if the keystone is removed, so does all the Church stand or fall with the truthfulness of the Book of Mormon. The enemies of the Church understand this clearly. This is why they go to such great lengths to try to disprove the Book of Mormon, for if it can be discredited, the Prophet Joseph Smith goes with it. So does our claim to priesthood keys, and revelation, and the restored Church. But in like manner, if the Book of Mormon be true—and millions have now testified that they have the witness of the Spirit that it is indeed true—then one must accept the claims of the Restoration and all that accompanies it.

Yes, my beloved brothers and sisters, the Book of Mormon is the keystone of our religion—the keystone of our testimony, the keystone of our doctrine, and the keystone in the witness of our Lord and Savior.

The *second* great reason why we must make the Book of Mormon a center focus of study is that it was written for our day. The Nephites never had the book; neither did the Lamanites of ancient times. It was meant for us. Mormon wrote near the end of the Nephite civilization. Under the inspiration of God, who sees all things from the beginning, he abridged centuries of records, choosing the stories, speeches, and events that would be most helpful to us.

Each of the major writers of the Book of Mormon testified that he wrote for future generations. Nephi said: "The Lord God promised unto me that these things which I write shall be kept and preserved, and handed down unto my seed, from generation to generation" (2 Nephi 25:21). His brother Jacob, who succeeded him, wrote similar words: "For [Nephi] said that the history of his people should be engraven upon his other plates, and that I should preserve these plates and hand them down unto my seed, from generation to generation" (Jacob 1:3). Enos and Jarom both indicated that they too were writing not for their own peoples but for future generations (see Enos 1:15–16; Jarom 1:2).

Mormon himself said, "Yea, I speak unto you, ye remnant of the house of Israel" (Mormon 7:1). And Moroni, the last of the inspired writers, actually saw our day and time. "Behold," he said, "the Lord hath shown unto me great and marvelous things concerning that which must shortly come, at that day when these things shall come forth among you.

"Behold, I speak unto you as if ye were present, and yet ye are not. But behold, Jesus Christ hath shown you unto me, and I know your doing" (Mormon 8:34–35).

If they saw our day, and chose those things which would be of greatest worth to us, is not that how we should study the Book of Mormon? We should constantly ask ourselves, "Why did the Lord inspire Mormon (or Moroni or Alma) to include that in his record? What lesson can I learn from that to help me live in this day and age?"

And there is example after example of how that question will be answered. For example, in the Book of Mormon we find a pattern for preparing for the Second Coming. A major portion of the book centers on the few decades just prior to Christ's coming to America. By careful study of that time period, we can determine why some were destroyed in the terrible judgments that preceded His coming and what brought others to stand at the temple in the land of Bountiful and thrust their hands into the wounds of His hands and feet.

From the Book of Mormon we learn how disciples of Christ live in times of war. From the Book of Mormon we see the evils of secret combinations portrayed in graphic and chilling reality. In the Book of Mormon we find lessons for dealing with persecution and apostasy. We learn much about how to do missionary work. And more than anywhere else, we see in the Book of Mormon the dangers of materialism and setting our hearts on the things of the world. Can anyone doubt that this book was meant for us and that in it we find great power, great comfort, and great protection?

The *third* reason why the Book of Mormon is of such value to Latter-day Saints is given in the same statement by the Prophet Joseph Smith cited previously. He said, "I told the brethren that the Book of Mormon was the most correct of any book on earth, and the keystone of our religion, and a man would get nearer to God by abiding by its precepts, than by any other book." That is the third reason for studying the book. It helps us draw nearer to God. Is there not something deep in our hearts that longs to draw nearer to God, to be more like Him in our daily walk, to feel His presence with us constantly? If so, then the Book of Mormon will help us do so, more than any other book.

It is not just that the Book of Mormon teaches us truth, though it indeed does that. It is not just that the Book of Mormon bears testimony of Christ, though it indeed does that, too. But there is something more. There is a power in the book which will begin to flow into your lives the moment you begin a serious study of the book. You will find greater power to resist temptation. You will find the power to avoid deception. You will find the power to stay on the strait and narrow path. The scriptures are called "the words of life" (see D&C 84:85), and nowhere is that more true than it is of the Book of Mormon. When you begin to hunger and thirst after those words, you will find life in greater and greater abundance.

Our beloved brother, President Marion G. Romney, who celebrated his eighty-ninth birthday last month and who knows of himself of the power that resides in this book, testified of the blessings that can come into the lives of those who will read and study the Book of Mormon. He said: "I feel certain that if, in our homes, parents will read from the Book of Mormon prayerfully and regularly, both by themselves and with their children, the spirit of that great book will come to permeate our homes and all who dwell therein. The spirit of reverence will increase; mutual respect and consideration for each other will grow. The spirit of contention will depart.

Parents will counsel their children in greater love
and wisdom. Children will be more responsive
and submissive to the counsel of their parents.
Righteousness will increase. Faith, hope, and
charity—the pure love of Christ—will abound in
our homes and lives, bringing in their wake peace,
joy, and happiness" (*Ensign*, May 1980, 67).

These promises—increased love and harmony
in the home, greater respect between parent and
child, increased spirituality and righteousness—
are not idle promises, but exactly what the
Prophet Joseph Smith meant when he said the
Book of Mormon will help us draw nearer to God.

Brethren and sisters, I implore you with all
my heart that you consider with great solemnity
the importance of the Book of Mormon to you
personally and to the Church collectively.

Over ten years ago I made the following statement regarding the Book of Mormon:

"Do eternal consequences rest upon our

response to this book? Yes, either to our blessing or our condemnation.

"Every Latter-day Saint should make the study of this book a lifetime pursuit. Otherwise he is placing his soul in jeopardy and neglecting that which could give spiritual and intellectual unity to his whole life. There is a difference between a convert who is built on the rock of Christ through the Book of Mormon and stays hold of that iron rod, and one who is not" (*Ensign*, May 1975, 65).

I reaffirm those words to you this day. Let us not remain under condemnation, with its scourge and judgment, by treating lightly this great and marvelous gift the Lord has given to us. Rather, let us win the promises associated with treasuring it up in our hearts.

In the Doctrine and Covenants, section 84, verses 54 to 58, we read:

"And your minds in times past have been

darkened because of unbelief, and because you have treated lightly the things you have received—

"Which vanity and unbelief have brought the whole church under condemnation.

"And this condemnation resteth upon the children of Zion, even all.

"And they shall remain under this condemnation until they repent and remember the new covenant, even the Book of Mormon and the former commandments which I have given them, not only to say, but to do according to that which I have written—

"That they may bring forth fruit meet for their Father's kingdom; otherwise there remaineth a scourge and judgment to be poured out upon the children of Zion."

Since last general conference, I have received many letters from Saints, both young and old, from all over the world who accepted the challenge to read and study the Book of Mormon.

I have been thrilled by their accounts of how their lives have been changed and how they have drawn closer to the Lord as a result of their commitment. These glorious testimonies have reaffirmed to my soul the words of the Prophet Joseph Smith that the Book of Mormon is truly "the keystone of our religion" and that a man and woman will "get nearer to God by abiding by its precepts, than by any other book."

This is my prayer, that the Book of Mormon may become the keystone of our lives, in the name of Jesus Christ, amen.

From an address given at the October 1986 general conference while President Benson was serving as president of The Church of Jesus Christ of Latter-day Saints (see *Ensign,* November 1986, 4–7).